Staying Abreast

Personal, inspirational, and reflective writings
presented by breast cancer survivors,
family, and friends

Written and Compiled by

Jeannette Kirchdoerfer Gardner

Staying Abreast

Jeannette Kirchdoerfer Gardner

Copyright © Jeannette Kirchdoerfer Gardner 2012

Published by 1st World Publishing
P.O. Box 2211, Fairfield, Iowa 52556
tel: 641-209-5000 • fax: 866-440-5234
web: www.1stworldpublishing.com

Revised Edition

LCCN: 2012914911
SoftCover ISBN: 978-1-4218-8652-7
HardCover ISBN: 978-1-4218-8653-4
eBook ISBN: 978-1-4218-8654-1

This material has been written and published for educational purposes to enhance one's wellbeing. In regard to health issues, the information is not intended as a substitute for appropriate care and advice from health professionals, nor does it equate to the assumption of medical or any other form of liability on the part of the publisher or author. The publisher and author shall have neither liability nor responsibility to any person or entity with respect to loss, damages or injury claimed to be caused directly or indirectly by any information in this book.

A % of the sales proceeds will be donated to breast cancer projects.

The Artist
Elizabeth Helen Hook

As a former teacher of hers, I am extremely honored that she has shared her artistic talent on the cover design and with the free-hand artwork throughout this book. Elizabeth, whatever path you choose, may you find peace and joy. At the age of thirteen Elizabeth's giftedness was clearly evident.

Contents

On Becoming

"With change taking place all around you, you've got to continue adjusting which means that you are going to constantly be becoming. There is no stopping. We're all on a fantastic journey! Every day is new. Every experience is new. Every person is new. Everything is new, every morning of your life."

—Leo Buscaglia (Author)

The late Dr. Leo Buscaglia, a leading educator, lecturer and writer, was one of my university instructors in 1964. Through the years I followed his teaching and embraced the power of the positive spirit which is so energizing. His books include: *Love; Living, Loving & Learning; Loving Each Other; Bus 9 to Paradise;* and *Born for Love: Reflections on Loving.*

—J. K. Gardner

Photographs by Jeannette K. Gardner

Dedication

To all breast cancer survivors and to those who belong to their loving support group.

To my dear, departed friends, Brenda and Jana, whose courage and positive attitudes led to incredible support for others. I will always remember the special times together and the laughter that was ours.

To Dr. Donald Armstrong for his thorough approach to medical care and deep concern for patients like me. There is great reason for hope.

Acknowledgement

To my husband and son...you were by my side from the beginning of this journey. In addition, you understood my passion for this project and let me find my way through it all. I thank you for being so compassionate.

To my parents and sisters...in your very own ways you showed me that love was the backbone to recovery. God bless you.

To my dear friend, Cathy Thomas...you strengthened me with love, laughter, and song. Thank you for taking care of me especially when I really needed it. I also appreciate your TLC with this book since the beginning.

To my neighbor, Anne Barbour...your creative flyers asking for contributions by breast cancer survivors, family members, and friends gave this project a terrific kick start. Thank you.

To my contributors...sharing your powerful experiences and thoughts through writing and art shows you have an extremely courageous nature. Without your support, this publication would not have happened. To you, I am deeply grateful and I thank you so very much.

To my readers...Shirlee Heidler, Marilyn Moody, Elizabeth Nelson, and Cathy Thomas, you are a blessing. Helping to narrow down the text from your different perspectives provided me with excellent guidance.

To my colleagues, Judy and Jim Crum...you gave countless hours to help me learn about computers and how to access information. You are so appreciated.

To my loyal friend, Elaine Hogue...your vision and support of my dream goes uncontested. I feel so humbled.

To Dona Garrish...we have walked many "paths" together. What a support you have been!

To Janice Carson and Michael Crook...your computer literacy means so much to me as does our friendship.

To all of my friends...I am thankful for your love and inspiration. We have been friends...in sunshine and shade.

To Dr. Gary Shumway...you gave me the confidence to be challenged with this project through your expertise during the first publishing.

To Dr. Allen Murray...Thank you for your support, patience, and guidance during my effort to republish this book.

To God...you have guided me through my healing and my commitment. We did it!!!

All my love, Jeannette

Reflections

We may not always realize that everything
we do,
Affects not only our lives, but touches others
too.
For a little bit of thoughtfulness that shows
someone you care,
Creates a ray of sunshine for both of you to
share.
Yes, every time you offer someone a helping
hand,
Every time you show a person you care and
understand,
Every time you have a kind and gentle word
to give,
You help someone find beauty in the precious
way we live.
For happiness brings happiness, and loving
ways bring love,
And giving is the treasure that contentment
is made of.

Author Unknown

Our Time

The shock is over concerning my wife's breast cancer. Counting our blessings, we write to honor and support the strong inspiration to love. No longer concerned about how it could have happened, we are committed to move on with wholesome living. Now is the time to emphasize relationships and to be giving. This is how we can show our appreciation for those who have given to us. This is our time.

We give thanks to the blessed doctors for their timely diagnosis, treatment, and guidance. Furthermore, we give thanks for the love and care by the staff and volunteers and from our family and friends.

Here is hoping the readers feel love and inspiration. Timing is everything! God bless.

Jerry R. Gardner (Husband)

To my beloved Mother, for all the courage and strength you have displayed in your triumph over breast cancer.

My admiration and respect for you has reached an even higher level since seeing you take this adverse condition and transform it into such a positive deed. May all those who read your collection of writings find hope and inspiration as they try to cope with the hardships of breast cancer. It is my belief that courage and strength can be found through love. I know... for that is where I found it.

Mom, I love you as big as the sky.

"Jefferson" Jeff Gardner (Son)

Author's Notes

In the evening, two days before my 50th birthday, THE telephone call came through informing me that the biopsied lump in my breast was indeed malignant. Fortunately, my husband was with me and together we were paralyzed with disbelief. However, several birthday surprises had been planned that weekend and were not cancelled. Yes, I really chose to CELEBRATE LIFE in the biggest way for three days!!!

Taking charge of my life, I sought many opinions, researched unanswered questions, and found peace of mind in my desire for quality of life. Loving support from my husband, son, other family members, and friends helped to give me the strength and determination to fight for my life.

During my recovery from my second surgery, I began writing and soon determined that an inspirational book would indeed be worthy of pursuing. For one year I collected personal, inspirational, and reflective writing and drawings by breast cancer survivors, family, and friends which I intended to collate into a special book.

This dream project which I became quite passionate about became a reality. My intentions are to not only share the writings, but to give comfort to those who are newly diagnosed with breast cancer, to use writing and art as a therapeutic tool toward recovery, and to support breast cancer programs. Because of the courageous support of the contributors, the following material is our gift to you.

Jeannette

Poetry, Passages, & Personal Essays

by Breast Cancer Survivors

Not Alone

The moment I told everyone that I had breast cancer, at least 25 women came up to tell me that they also had cancer and mastectomies 5, 10, and 15 years ago and were doing just fine! That is when it really hit me how, unfortunately, common breast cancer really was. Also that I was not alone! From that moment on, I began to regain my emotional strength. The shock started to subside. I began to make plans, and very importantly, my sense of humor started to re-emerge.

1. If I need chemotherapy and my hair falls out to where I resemble Yul Brenner, I'll go for the blonde wig.

2. Chemotherapy does wonders for getting rid of facial hair.

3. Just think of it - millions of women, every year, spend millions of dollars on cosmetics and surgery to look young again through tummy tucks, breast implants, etc. Yet, in just one great swoop, here I am having a silhouette of a 12 year old girl! The only problem is, is that the side of me that has no breast wants to go through puberty again, but the opposite side of me says, "No way!"

Miriam Handel

A Prayer of Thanksgiving

As the sun shines down on Maui
and glistens on the sea,
I feel its warmth from deep within
and blessed abundantly.
The two past years before this
my life was so uncertain,
with cancer, anger, fear, and pain
drawn over me like a curtain.
I struggled and I cried
and I prayed to God above.
And He looked down and smiled at me
and showered me with love.
From family, friends, and those unknown,
from far and near came prayers.
God heard everyone I know
He healed and removed my cares.
And now on top of all His blessings
He's given me much more -
these beautiful tropical islands
and the sands upon their shore,
the azure skies, the billowy clouds,
the sweetest scent of flowers
the gentle air against my face, and
refreshing sudden showers.
All of this and so much more
has filled these past eight days.
And I'm so thankful for it all
and God's healing, loving ways!

Judy Parker

A Cancer Survivor

As I sit and look at a picture of my two daughters, I thank God for the early warning of my breast cancer detection. I had felt a lump on my left breast that appeared suddenly and remained for a month. My doctor reacted quickly and sent me for a mammogram. The result, to my surprise, was cancer. Although uncertain and uneducated to the seriousness of my condition, I did what I was instructed to do. Confiding in my family, my friends, and my doctors, all those concerned guided me in seeking the right treatment for my condition.

My oncologist informed me that most individuals with my type of cancer treatment continued to work. But my decision was to stay home. As a working mom, this was my chance to be home for my daughters. Reflecting on my youth, knowing that when I came home from school, my mother and grandmother were always home waiting. I wanted my daughters to know the experience and cherish the memory.

As a wife and a mother handling multiple tasks, I focused my strengths and diversity toward the caring of my family. Until one day my Creator stepped in. He stepped in to tell me I couldn't do it without Him. It was His calling against my invisibility that made me realize it is He we turn to for comfort and guidance in our most desperate time of need.

I've been in remission for nearly three years and I thank God for each day that I live. I know, for me personally, God is keeping close.

Susanna Revilla

Photo Essay

There is a picture of a woman with long full hair, a slight smile crosses her lips. It is the smile of innocence. Unbeknownst to her, there is cancer growing in her left breast.

There is a picture of a woman who wears her baldness in defiance. Her smile is one of hope.

There is a picture of a woman who has fuzz on her head and young children at her side. Her smile is one of thankfulness.

There is a picture of a woman with a mass of chemo curls. Her smile is one of pure joy.

Denise Kalures Shuger

The Race

It's been three days since this year's Race, yet the overwhelming feeling of sisterhood is still with me. Last year when I did the Race I could not stay for the Survivor's Ceremony because I had done the 5K walk, and I was under chemotherapy. How I did that walk I'll never know, but I went home after it was done and crashed out on my bed.

Two years ago, I was diagnosed with breast cancer. Before that time I admit that I had not been involved with the fight against this disease. You see, breast cancer was something that happened to other women, but not to me - or so I thought back then. So, in my first Race I was skinny and pale and missing some hair from chemotherapy, but there was no way that I was going to miss out on participation in something as necessary as raising money for a cure.

During that Race, I was brought to tears throughout the 5K walk. They were brought on by the pink signs worn on the backs of other racers in memory of loved ones. As I read each one, new tears would come into my eyes. Even now, as I type, they come again. It was what I called a "bitter - sweet" experience. We all have lost too many loved ones from this disease.

This past year went by quickly. I became more involved with breast cancer issues and made a lot of friends with other breast cancer women. Believe me, I found this to be one sisterhood that cannot be ignored.

In the last part of this year's Survivor Ceremony was another pink sign on the back of a walker which had words that are now branded in my mind. It was worn by a lady who had very little hair. We all knew she was there while undergoing her chemotherapy. Her pink sign read, "My grandmother died from breast cancer. My mother died from breast cancer. I will run, walk, or crawl for a cure so that my daughter does not have to go through this, too."

Marilyn Moody

My Thoughts on Surviving Breast Cancer

My name is Sharon. I have been a breast cancer survivor for two years. I am also an oncology nurse. Working in a chemotherapy treatment room and administering chemotherapy to oncology patients in an outpatient setting helps me to form a special bond between all of my cancer patients and myself. They know I've "been through it" too, and that I understand the fears and concerns.

Recently, I sat down and put my many thoughts about my cancer experience in a journal. It is a record of how I coped, and where I had difficulties. These are the many thoughts I share with my patients, when appropriate. I would like to share them with you.

My thoughts on having a mastectomy:

Yes, I was angry, frightened, and sad. I cried and raged, but then I knew I would do what I had to do... for LIFE is too precious. (A lumpectomy was not medically appropriate for me.)

I had a mastectomy with an immediate TRAM flap reconstruction. That's where they do a "tummy tuck" and use the fat and muscle to reconstruct the breast mound. I got a flat stomach and two boobs out of the deal!

It was so important to me to have the immediate reconstruction. When I woke up, I still had two breasts. Yes, I have scars, but I never felt that part of me was missing; it just got rearranged!

I love my new figure! I went from size 10 to size 6. I wear cuter and "sexier" clothes now. My husband and family love my new image.

My thoughts on chemotherapy:

* It's not a lot of fun, but it's "do-able."

*The alternative is not very appealing.

* I figured, "I'm Supernurse. I'll just breeze

through chemo. It won't slow me down!" Wrong! I did slow down.

* I used to go to bed before the kids did!

* It takes a long time to get over the fatigue. Give yourself six months to a year, and be patient! It will get better!

My thoughts on hair:

* My hair came out thirteen days after my first course of chemo. The worst part about your hair falling out is that you have to clean it up—everywhere! It's disgusting! You don't know how much hair you have until it falls out.

* On the plus side, I only had to shave my legs every other week. Doing my "hair" was a snap. I just put my wig on. I could sleep fifteen minutes longer in the morning. In fact, I got so spoiled, I've kept my hair cut short since it grew back because it's so easy.

* My kids said I'd make a great 'alien' on Star Trek. Every time a bald-headed lady alien was on the show, they said, "Mom, you could do that!" Gee, thanks!

* Body hair also goes. I hadn't looked like that since I was twelve! I had a great bikini line, but I found out one use for pubic hair—without it you can't pee straight! It goes every which way. Ugh!

* Facial hair thins—my complexion never looked so smooth! People said I looked younger!

My thoughts on growing hair again:

* I never thought I could spend so much time admiring "peach fuzz" in the mirror.

* One of my greatest pleasures was feeling the breeze ruffle MY hair!

My thoughts on radiation:

* Getting radiation is a "piece of cake" compared to chemo. However, the side effects can sneak up on you after you finish.

My thoughts on getting on with life:

* It's very difficult to stop thinking about having cancer—even though mine was caught very early, before it had spread.

* You need to be very patient with yourself. It takes a long time to recover. Give yourself at least a year!

The only time I got depressed was after all my treatments were finished. All of a sudden, I wasn't *doing* anything to fight the cancer. I felt, "There's nothing to do but wait and see if it comes back." These feelings are very common and go away in time. Of course, there is something to "do." You can get on with your life.

It helps to stay busy. My children are wonderful. They expect me to be "normal," and I can't disappoint them. I still resent the fact that I'll have to be concerned about cancer the rest of my life; there are no guarantees. But I'll not dwell on it. Probably the best thing I learned from my cancer experience was just how many friends I have and how much people care. That kind of support is invaluable. It still amazes me to think of how many people are out there that love me!

Sharon Reed

The Wrap Up

Six months of chemo can seem pretty depressing, so to give myself some lighter moments I had a little fun with my medical bills. When a computer printout of my bill from the oncologist proved to be twenty-one feet long, I knew I had to do something creative with it! I wrapped myself "mummy-like" in the bill and asked a friend to photograph me. We sent the photo to the First Lady supporting her interest in health care and received a gracious reply. We visual artists often see absurdities in life as a creative challenge!

Jo Raksin

The Shadow

For the first time during my chemo treatments, I went alone to the oncologist's office. This was by design, in part because I had been turned down a treatment the previous time as my blood levels had been too low and there was usually much waiting time in offices. Believe me, the disappointment of not moving on in my treatments was tremendous. In the past, my husband, son, and/or friend had spent many hours waiting with me to comfort me, to humor me, or to quietly say I love you.

On this given day, while I visited with the nurse awaiting the results of my pre-treatment blood test, out of the corner of my eye, I sensed a figure at my right side. I looked upward from the legs in shorts to an incredibly beautiful, smiling face. My son!!! I stood. We kissed. We hugged.

Jeff, who had known about this appointment, had seriously wanted to be with me and drove home from college in LA even though he had a hectic schedule that day. Needless to say, he was not happy about my being alone for this treatment.

After this encounter I made a promise that someone would be by my side from then on for further treatments. Although I was again denied a treatment that day, the memory of this powerfully moving experience will long be remembered.

Lunch, a kiss good-bye...we parted.

Jeannette K. Gardner

Bluebirds of Happiness

In mid-October of last year, a few days before my 51st birthday, a biopsy was performed on the lump I had only known about for three weeks. A few days after my birthday, my surgeon phoned me and told me that it was cancer. This didn't come as a shock; he had even asked on the day of the biopsy if I wanted to be told the results in person or on the phone, and he had prepared my husband and me for the very strong possibility of cancer. His caring attitude came through in his voice. Still, at first, I wondered what kind of a birthday present this was. Then my thoughts turned to the positive. . .how lucky I was to know that I had a problem, and to have help with the problem.

I had been healthy all of my life…no operations, no broken bones. It felt unreal…yet not totally unreal. There had been several other cases of cancer in my family, including breast cancer. My grandmother had had a mastectomy more than 50 years ago, at a time when nobody spoke of these things. However, these were the 90's (in fact, it was Breast Cancer Awareness Month), and there was a great deal of publicity everywhere about the disease, how curable it had become, and how many other women had been through this.

Given the options of a modified radical mastectomy or a partial mastectomy, I decided on the modified radical mastectomy, partly because of my family history. Surgery was scheduled for October 31. I couldn't help thinking that Halloween was a strange day to have surgery. But Thanksgiving was coming.

On November 4, three days home from the hospital, I wrote, "Everyone says you should keep a journal of how it feels and what you go through when you have cancer. To be very honest, I hope I don't have it anymore, that my operation took care of the whole thing. Right now, I will just wait until they can tell me more. My first priority now is to let my body heal, so that I can move freely and not worry about pulling stitches, or that some sudden movement will cause injury. I've had this feeling that I'm going through the strangest experience of my life. I've looked in the mirror and smiled, seeing myself almost young and carefree. My daughter said the reason I feel this way is that so many people have been praying for me, even people at her school that I have never met. All those prayers do have their effect. I never realized how really powerful so many prayers added together can be."

Prayers, beautiful plants and flowers from the office and family, gifts of angels, sincere wishes written in get-well cards, frequent phone conversations with my parents in Northern California, all have helped. Being open about the cancer with friends and family was the right decision.

I met my oncologist. Like most people I have talked with who haven't had experience with cancer, I didn't know until I had it what an oncologist was, or the difference between chemotherapy and radiation. I have learned from books, and especially from the many healthcare professionals in every aspect of diagnosis and treatment who have helped me. The oncologist gave me the good news (cancer didn't get to the lymph nodes) and then the bad news (the cancer was very aggressive, and a few other points). He was prescribing six treatments of chemotherapy, but the milder type that would probably cause only minimal hair loss as a side effect.

Minimal hair loss... that was nice. I talked to my mother on the phone, and she immediately put me on the mailing lists for wig catalogs and sent me money to buy two wigs. I thought she was being extreme... Didn't I say "minimal" hair loss!

Mothers (sometimes) know best, even when you're 51 years old! As it turned out, my oncologist changed the treatment plan, after talking more with the pathologist and studying details. My cancer was closer to the chest wall than he had previously thought, and there might be some stray cells remaining. He was now suggesting radiation, and also the stronger of the two combinations of chemotherapy drugs that he had been considering. This change to stronger chemo would mean I'd lose my hair (not "minimal," but "total"). Mom was right. I needed a wig catalog. Having found an excellent choice of wigs in the catalogue my mother sent and having found nothing I liked in stores, I called, ordered a wig to be rushed to me, and received it in just a few days.

December 8 was my first chemo treatment, and about a week before Christmas my hair (or maybe that's really the scalp) was hurting when I walked in the wind. How could wind blow your hair enough to make it hurt? My hair was coming out.

The day after Christmas I went to the mall *with my own hair*. The next day, a work day, I couldn't have appeared in public without my new wig. It happened that fast. As time moved forward, the six chemotherapy treatments were given three weeks apart. Less than two weeks after my last treatment (March 24), my hair started to grow again.

Today, two months later, I'm still wearing the wig. . .maybe for a few more months. I've never liked wearing anything on my head, but it's the only thing I'm comfortable with in public. It's fairly short, similar to my own hair at its normal length. I really don't think that hair is a very important part of this whole subject, but it does give a new perspective and makes a person appreciate hair that stays attached and doesn't just "de-anchor" itself at will.

Chemotherapy wasn't easy, but that's over now. The nurses were always friendly and helpful, doing a precise and serious job in the most professional way possible. I'm still in the middle of treatment; this time, radiation. There are 25 radiation treatments in all. Right now it's 15 down with 10 to go. I am thankful there is radiation and that there are dedicated experts to operate the equipment.

Except for three weeks that I spent at home right after the operation, I have been able to keep working. Talking to people has helped. Paying attention to good nutrition has helped. Someone suggested water aerobics for exercise; I ended up swimming laps instead (between chemotherapy treatments, but not during radiation). It felt wonderful, and I intend to start doing it again as soon as the radiation is over.

My thanks to all the healthcare professionals who have helped me over the past eight months. There have been many, starting with the nurse practitioner who detected the lump. Although she didn't know if it was cancer, she gave me her best wishes and had a very caring attitude about my future. I hope to be able to pass it along to others.

Thanks also to my husband, our son, and our two daughters who have all shown so much love.

Thanks to opera, beautiful white water birds and bluebirds of happiness, ducks on a pond, Yosemite, Machu Picchu, London. Being a dreamer isn't all that bad.

Dianne Corzo

Healing Me

During the days of my radiation, the staff members working on me would all come in and see how I was doing. They checked to see what was new. When I was in the room alone, knowing I was alone, I always felt like each one of the ladies who had talked to me, who had been considerate and thoughtful, had her hands on me and she was healing me. *It wasn't lonely and it wasn't frightening.*

Jeanette Sherman

Mounds

The plastic surgeon
calls them breasts.
I say breasts, too,
but it feels like lying.

My lover knows the truth–
there is form
but no function.
Why then does he still

want to touch?
Even after making love,
he rests his hand there,
his fingers curved, relaxed.

I wonder if he needs
this shape as much as I.
Is this familiar roundness,
like that of fruit

the earth
the moon
what we see of the sky
a source of some comfort?

Lizbeth Parker

Taking Action

I have been active in speaking out publicly about my experience with breast cancer and want to support any effort that helps women help themselves.

In the process of doing a three-part series on my breast cancer experience on our local TV talk show, I discussed wigs and their uses to name a few. AND I went so far as to change wigs on camera. It was a real "TV moment." Even though I had told the talk show hostess I would do it, I think she didn't really believe me until it happened. But I thought... what a better way to break out of the self-imposed embarrassment that many of us feel about losing our hair than to take the strong position of not only not trying to hide my baldness, but willingly exposing it. Believe me, I felt strong, not weak, in taking that action.

Peggy Vaughan

From Nature

The beautiful mountains
  capped with snow,
The desert and the blue sage
  we know.
The dew on the grass
  the sunlight's bright gleam,
The wonderful
  quiet calm like a dream.
The bounding deer
  just a flicker of brown,
The glide of the eagle,
  the ridge and lake renown.
The swiftness of water
  the sway of a tree,
The vast out-of-doors
  the birds that fly free.
The sun going down
  and the night coming on,
The colors of sky,
  the birds' sleepy song.
The greatness of the valleys
  the way shadows grow,
The twinkle of
  lights that fade and glow.
The peeping stars
  soon to grow bright,
The wonder of day,
  the wonder of night.

Laura I. Delano

Positives

Breast cancer has been a negative, as well as a positive experience for me: the positives such as living with a greater emotional awareness and appreciation of each day and its experiences. Some friends who remained faithful through the turmoil were definite positives. So I now know who my *true* friends are, and I now have a greater bond with them. The best positive in my life is my husband, who has remained a constant support by being my friend, emotional counselor, and who has been actively involved in nearly everything that I do. For the positive results of this disease, I am thankful!

Janet K. Butcher

Hope

What has helped me keep hope has been my family's love, my doctors who have been so caring, and reading my bible. Also, when I go to my support group, I find out there are so many of us survivors.

Anna Vaughan

Guardian Angel

In recalling a memory, there was the last night in the hospital. It was around 1:30 A.M.

I woke up crying and there was a nurse who held me in her arms, talking softly, and kind of rocking me like I was a baby. I don't know how long it was before she left, because I fell back to sleep. I never saw her again. I didn't know her name. I wanted to thank her. Yet truthfully, I think she was my guardian angel whom I will never forget.

Anna Vaughan

"47"

I look like a walking stick and am taking life today, one day at a time.
On the brighter side I did something I've always wanted to do... learn
to ride a motorcycle. I did! I got my license and, of course, a new 1200
candy apple red sportster, Harley Davidson. So, see, there is life after
breast cancer. Oh, I'll be 47 next month!!!

Anna Vaughan

High Dose

Cells Harvested,
Body Cleansed, and
Cancer Free.
Vitamins Back,
Cells Back.
A New Life For Me.

Deanna Washer

The Next Step in the Journey

I can still look back and see myself in those dreadful moments on March 5, the shock of my first breast cancer diagnosis. Three and a half years later a recurrence and the terrible news that I would need to lose my right breast. I can reach back over the years and touch an echo of the terror...the great fear that I might die because my cancer had come back. The even greater fear was that I might live... being so changed by my surgery that I would be unlovable, undesirable, untouchable forever after.

It is now eleven years since my last surgery, and I do frequently look back. But now, the fear has been replaced with an enormous feeling of gratitude and pride as I compare who I was then with whom I have become.

Breast cancer has been a powerful catalyst in my own personal growth. The best thing that ever happened to me? Not by a long shot! Even today, knowing what I have gained, I would not choose this experience. *I still find myself wishing sometimes that I could have learned any life-lessons in some other, gentler ways.* But if breast cancer hasn't been one of the best things that ever happened to me, it has certainly been one of the most important, not because it is inherently a wonderful event, but because of how I was able to use it to learn and to grow.

As I look back on my own process of recovery and the subsequent work I have done with so many other women with breast cancer, a few issues seem to stand out as pivotal in the healing process. The resolution of these issues not only hastens ones recovery, but turns out to have enormous impact in all the other areas of our lives.

To begin with, it is vital that we not let people tell us how we should feel. I learned to say, "If I'm feeling this, there's a very good reason, even if I don't know what the reason is right at this moment!" With a little patience and a little detective work, the reason always surfaces eventually. Going through cancer recovery is unknown territory for most of us. As we make our way through, we are sometimes hindered by unfair and undeserved judgment and criticism from others. Even well-meant advice from people who don't understand this journey can throw us off balance. We also have to be careful not to judge ourselves, not to set up unrealistic standards for what we **should** feel or how quickly we **should** recover. *We are the experts on how we feel, not family, not friends, not doctors! No one has to solve our feelings for us, because feelings cannot be solved.* We are allowed to tell our truths and have those truths respected. What we need is validation - from others and from ourselves. We don't need people to fix our feelings, only to hold our hand sometimes and keep us company as we journey. Obviously, if we can learn this lesson in relation to breast cancer, we can apply it to life in general in a way that can be very freeing.

Next, most women are wonderful givers. After all we have been groomed to be the caretakers, the nurturers. Many women going through a breast cancer experience find it terribly uncomfortable to ask for help. After years of serving others, we have trouble even defining, much less communicating our needs. There seems to be some embarrassment or shame attached. Learning to ask for support and help and learning to borrow power from others when we are feeling weak and needy may seem humbling at first. However, until we can receive from others as graciously as we can give, we are living in a state of imbalance. While we are designed to face challenges in life, we were never meant to face them alone!

For me, body image was another major issue. How could anyone love me when I was so changed by my mastectomy, I wondered. How could I love myself? What I have discovered is that I had bought society's values without ever questioning whether they were right for me. The current definition of sexy seems to be 'under 35, over 5'7", less than 115 pounds, and definitely two breasted. I don't fit into even one of those categories. Healing involved tearing myself away from society's stereotypes, getting in touch with my essence, and discovering that all that I am is safe deep inside me. Surgery can't touch it, aging can't touch it, even the opinions of others can't touch it. Today, when I look at my body, I see an Amazon woman. Today, when I look at my scar, I see a badge that says **"survivor."**

I feel sexy, feminine, attractive, and sensual, and because I feel that way, the men in my life have seen me that way as well.

Finally, I had to confront a complex of issues that seem to be common for so many of us when we are diagnosed with a life-threatening illness: fear of recurrence, fear of death, mortality and vulnerability. How can we live well knowing that life is limited? How can we invest in the future if we have no guarantee of having a future? If we only have a limited time on earth, what is it that makes life meaningful? These are just a few of the vitally important questions that surfaced. The answers have not come in a sudden flash, but rather over the years as an ongoing process. Developing a mature spirituality, one that would support me in times of crisis, has been one result of being challenged in this way. Shifting my perspective on what makes life meaningful has been another. I used to think that we were supposed to leave monuments behind, reminding future generations of our importance. Now, *I know that the purpose of life is to dedicate ourselves to our own growth and to touch other souls with kindness.* I understand that even before breast cancer there were no guarantees. That is simply part of the human condition. Therefore, I invest passionately in life because I refuse to sit around waiting for death. For those of you who are afraid to invest, ask yourselves the question, "What if I live?" I believe that living a conscious, purposeful life is the way to win against cancer. Knowing that I won't live forever, I look for value in each day.

The lessons have been good ones, powerful ones, important ones and I'm still learning. Breast cancer is no longer a tragedy, just a fact. So far, it has been a fascinating journey.

Ronnie Kaye

Ronnie Kaye is a psychotherapist and the author of *Spinning Straw into Gold: your emotional recovery from breast cancer* (Simon & Schuster, 1991)

Points to Ponder

1. Trust in your own good judgment.

2. Line from the 23rd Psalm and Betty Ford: It says, "You walk through the shadow of death. It does not say you have to stay there."

3. Reasons I can't die:

   a. Can't be bothered.

   b. Too busy!

   c. Being a zoologist, I have two grandsons who need to know about opossums (my specialty!).

   d. I want to live. I am alive and I want and hope it will stay that way!

   e. I am not alone - remember the women of the support group. They are marvelous.

4. I have gained a greater appreciation of life. I will help others, whenever I can, to overcome their fears, to let them know that they are definitely not alone! Most of all, together **we all** will help them conquer their cancers.

5. When we must have medication through an IV tube, visualize the IV tube, not as a tube, but as a second umbilical cord, because it, too, is giving us life!

Miriam Handel

A Breast Cancer Quandary

I considered my surgeon the best
Until he was put to the test,
For it was plain to see
We just couldn't agree,
He was planning to take off my breast!

The crux of this problem's not simple
It all seems to stem from my nipple,
How I want it to stay
But He'll take it away,
As if he were squeezing a pimple!

To these facts I will firmly attest
This woman's attached to her breast,
It's so hard to depart
From what's close to my heart,
So this surgery I surely contest!

He told me there'd be a revision
If I chose the wrong incision.
He'd see me no more
Of this I was sure,
Now I ask, "Was this a decision?"

I considered this surgery elective,
So I thought I could be more selective.
I reviewed all the facts
Till my emotions were taxed,
I just couldn't be objective!

On knees I went to God in despair
All my worries I pleaded in prayer,
And He gave me such peace
That my fears I released,
And replaced them with His loving care!

Judy Parker

Life ...What A Treasure

Acclaim it
Behold it
Cherish, challenge, celebrate it
Dream of defying the odds
Expand your knowledge; examine your past
Fathom what "it's" all about
Give of yourself to others
Honor life with a positive attitude
Inspire those in need
Join with loved ones and friends
Kindle and protect life
Learn to love with all your heart
Manage yourself
Never take life for granted
Open up the senses and smell the roses
Prepare for each day
Quiet the turmoil
Respect God's gift
Savor life's secrets
Tangle with life's diversities; tame stress
Understand life's friends and foes
View life with curiosity
Wander unknown paths
Xamine and prioritize your options
Yearn for peace of mind
Zero in on quality of life

Jeannette K. Gardner

More Thoughts From Miriam

*Imagine chasing your wig down the street on a windy day!

*There have been times when I wanted to put my wig on a leash and take it to the nearest tree to do its business!

*When the wind blows your wig off and someone remarks, "Oh, you have lost your hair!" You answer with a smile and say, "Now you see the real me!" and "Boy, am I beautiful!"

*There is something to be said about a bald head - a sense of freedom - it tingles! You can always "draw" curls all over your head with washable marker pens, if you wish, and any color you want! You can also get someone to draw eyes on the back and sides of your head with the caption, "I'm watching you, so don't try anything!"

*There is a relationship between a full moon and a bald head. Both have a lumpy, bumpy surface, but hopefully, only one has rocks in it!!

*I once had forgotten to secure my prosthesis in my bra with a safety pin before going grocery shopping. As I left the market, carrying packages, I felt the prosthesis slip out of the bra and down to my waist. Luckily, I caught it before it fell out of my blouse. Later on, while thinking about this incident, what if the prosthesis really did fall out and hit the ground? Can you imagine the reaction of a man, as he would try to pick it up for me and I yell at him, "Take your bloody hands off my breast!"?

Miriam Handel

No Need to Worry

During my experience with breast cancer I could be prone to 'worry'. I came across quotes and kept them around for reading if I started worrying. When I read the quotes my perspective would change. I would take a deep breath and was reminded – still am – that I do have control of my life by having a healthier frame of mind. The quotes below are a few of my favorites:

No Benefit to Worry

"If a problem is fixable, if a situation is such that you can do something about it, then there is no need to worry. If it's not fixable then there is no help in worrying. There is no benefit in worrying whatsoever."

—Dalai Lama XIV

Birds Don't Worry

"Therefore I tell you, do not worry about your life, what you will eat or drink; or about your body, what you will wear. Is not life more than food, and the body more than clothes? Look at the birds of the air; they do not sow or reap or store away in barns, and yet your heavenly Father feeds them. Are you not much more valuable than they? Can any one of you by worrying add a single hour to your life?

—Matthew 6:25

Sunlight

"Do not anticipate trouble, or worry about what may never happen. Keep in the sunlight."

—Benjamin Franklin

Julie Walsh Warcheski

Getting On

As I sit here on this rainy day at my computer, thinking, I am trying to put together the past. I feel I have successfully put the past at rest, knowing and hanging onto my oncologist's words, "Cancer is behind you now, so it is time to get on with the business of living."

I find that the first thing that comes to mind is the strength I drew on through the prayers, support and love of my family and friends. That, above all, was what got me through those dark days of my breast cancer operations, a radical mastectomy of the right breast.

I can't reproduce the prayers or the loving care or the support that was given to me, but I can share the saying on the card a friend sent to me, 'You can't turn back the clock, but you can wind it up again.' I have the card on my mirror and look at it each morning.

And that's what I'm doing...

Phyllis M. Sheue

Wit

God gave me a sense of

Humor,

A few small lumps and a

Tumor.

On the pitty-potty do I

Sit?

Nope, I choose to exercise my

Wit!

Deanna Washer

T.O.T.D.

If you cry all over a paper towel, it will be soft

enough to blow your nose on.

Deanna Washer

About Friends

One of my greatest discoveries through my illness and healing process has been the heightened awareness of the value of friendship. I soon realized that through constant support of card, phone calls and food that my worth was constantly being re-enforced and the strength and comfort I received by friends aided my healing process.

I always valued my friends and made an effort to cultivate relationships but I thought of them as fun people to drink coffee with and share the conversation of the day. Their value took on a new dimension as they were so attentive through my breast cancer experience. I believe I could actually feel physical strength as they reached out to me.

As a legacy from my wonderful and caring mother, I had always put other people's wishes and needs before mine, but now I was faced with a dread disease and had to make many serious decisions. At that particular time, I found myself very "self-centered' and wished to be isolated. I was surprised and overwhelmed by my friends' constant outreach. Sometimes we cried, sometimes laughed, but they were always there for me to pour out my heart to.

I shall always be thankful to Gary, my family and friends for making the difficult times tolerable. I know now I'll always take extra time to send a card, make that phone call or take that casserole, as I realize the importance of feeling that other people care. I hope I'm able to give back just a little of what I received.

Monica Helzer

Claim Your Dreams

In May I was diagnosed with breast cancer. When the doctor first told me, I was disbelieving and in shock. It didn't seem that this could be happening to me. I was not someone who got this type of disease. This was something that happened to other women, but not to me. I was young. I was skinny. I was active. I was healthy. No. No. No. This was all wrong. I was also very naive.

I thought…I don't have time to deal with any type of cancer. This was an annoyance and an inconvenience. I liked being in control and I liked the way my life was prior to breast cancer.

At this same time, I continued to write almost daily letters to my best friend since childhood. I began writing letters to her on a word processing program and saved a copy of each letter. Even though we lived far apart, she was my main support person.

After surgery I had more free time on my hands than in the past. Consequently, I kept compiling my letters to my friend into a manuscript. You see, I had always had a secret fantasy of being a published author. Of course, there was a doubting voice inside me saying that this was foolish thinking, so I had never seriously pursued my dream.

I'm grateful because what I finally learned from my cancer experience is to not wait, or to think negatively about any of my dreams. Cancer has taught me how to live and also to go after my most heartfelt desires now. Life is too short and I want to enjoy each precious day as fully as I can.

Remember that manuscript? Well, it grew and was sold last December when it was only half written. I had a difficult time accepting that anyone would consider reading something I had written. So, now I refuse to stop.

If I could just share one of my thoughts with all of you, it would be: Don't wait until you are facing your own mortality to go after your dreams. Grab onto them now. They are right here waiting for you to claim them.

Marilyn Moody

Marilyn has authored a book entitled *Courage & Cancer A Breast Cancer Diary, A Journey from Cancer to Cure*. (Rhache Publishing, Ltd.)

My Father's Hands

My mother takes me to the hospital
She sees me into, then out
of surgery, helps me through
not the first or last, but current pain.
She cools my face with damp towels
and badgers the nurse for morphine.
At my house, my father waits
the only way he knows. He builds
a shelf beside my bed, makes
leaves for my dining room table.

A week later, we eat breakfast
on the patio. I am not dying
today. We talk of practicalities,
the logistics of getting me
to and from treatment. I worry
about the bills piling up
after only a month. My father says,
"We'll help you. You must know
that if we couldn't we'd be desolate."
I think "desolate"? And yet somehow
it is the right word - a cross
between desperate and inconsolable.

My mother changes my dressings,
brings me shaved ice
when nothing else stays down.
My father builds for me a fireplace.
It will have a hearth, and a mantle

from oak already older than I.
From my bedroom, I hear the tap tap
of trowel handle as he levels each brick.
I picture his hands and their rhythm
with brick and mortar. Scoop, fling,
tap tap, scrape around, fling. Lulled
by the certain rhythm of my father
laying brick, I sleep. Scoop, fling,
tap tap, scrape around, fling.

My father heals the only way he knows.
He builds things to last me a lifetime.

Lizbeth Parker

My Tram Reconstruction

From the very day I had my mastectomy, I wanted to just go back to looking like I had before the operation. That's all I wanted, day and night! I was miserable. I tried to explain this need to my doctor. I thought he was going to tell me that I could have a saline implant like my friend had but no such luck. Because I had radiation and my skin wouldn't stretch, he said that I would have to have a Tram Flap Reconstruction. What in the world was that?

A Tram Flap Reconstruction consists of moving skin, fat and muscle from another part of the body to the mastectomy site. This was much more complex than I thought. I would have to find out more about it and think about it for awhile. I wanted someone to tell me I wouldn't have to do this. No luck! It was this way or nothing.

One of the plastic surgeons, Dr. "D", was special. She saw me several times and was very patient dealing with my hopes and fears. Then there were the other women who had had this surgery and always my positive friend encouraging me to have the surgery. I thought about it, investigated it, asked questions - but I was still scared. After all I didn't want to have this surgery - or did I? YES! I did have to have it. I didn't want to live in the body I was in. It was the only way out. I scheduled my surgery for eight weeks away so I could think about it some more - maybe change my mind???

Then one night I got a message on my answering machine. It was Dr. "D", the plastic surgeon who was going to do my surgery. She said she had been approached by the Learning Channel regarding filming a Tram reconstruction. She wanted to know if I would be willing to have my surgery filmed. Wow!! The pros and cons were flying through my mind. To help others by letting women know what was available would help make the whole experience of my cancer and my surgery more positive. Yet, this type of surgery was kind of private. Maybe too private for TV. Dr. "D" was interested in doing the show because she wanted to draw attention to this procedure as insurance companies were trying to classify reconstruction as plastic surgery. That would mean women with mastectomies wouldn't have the option for reconstruction because most of them couldn't afford to pay for this themselves. I was contacted by the producer and director of the show. They sent me tapes of previous shows - from a kidney transplant to a vasectomy. The format of the program was very professional with approximately five minutes with the patient before the surgery and then five minutes after the surgery. This looked like it might be fun. Something positive. Something I had never done before. I would learn how they filmed a TV show. Everyone associated with the show was so nice and friendly. So, *I agreed.* It was approximately four weeks after the surgery before I started feeling better. I had been in pain, stiff, and tired from the day of surgery. It was a little better everyday, but it wasn't easy. Was it worth it? *YES! YES! YES!* I can bend over without worrying about it. I can wear low cut clothes. Plus in front of the mirror or in the shower, I look more feminine.

I finally feel something good has come out of my breast cancer experience. I feel like I have progressed out of the deep abyss of despair I once felt. I have made progress. I am on my way.

Jean Dubravac

From Fear to Strength

During a visit to my vacation home on the Hawaiian island of Kauai, I was overwhelmed by a very strong inner-personal awareness. I realized that my own physical and emotional strength, now being challenged by the destructive force of cancer, closely paralleled the trail of devastation that challenged the natural beauty of the island paradise by the forces of the storm, *Iniki*.

Soon after, a more beautiful parallel was realized. The strength of my own determination, a determination for life, was successfully delivering me from the grasp of the disease.

Today, my life and my art reflect the healing of body, mind, and soul. The blending of canvas and color symbolize my personal re-growth and revival of spirit, just as nature has done so beautifully for Kauai. The landscape is once again blooming, the sandy beaches are clean, and the birds are finally back. Kauai and I are *enduring and triumphant!*

Paula Bramlett

Summer of My Life

I'm hanging onto Summer
While Fall comes slipping in.
Can't accept the thought of Winter
Anticipating Spring again.

Deanna Washer

Chemo Curls

Every time I start to cut my hair
My right elbow goes weak.
And I say, "It's not so bad. I've got hair.
I'll wait until next week."

Deanna Washer

Bone Marrow Transplant

The most interesting aspect of my long journey with cancer has been the path I chose as my experience. There was no questioning the diagnosis; I saw the bone scan. This began my personal challenge. You see, the original diagnosis of breast cancer was coming back to visit me as bone cancer.

This time I needed to make more changes in my thinking, eating, goals, habits, and what I began to ask from others. Meditation, for me had come to mean a totally relaxed body. Even today, practice has guided me to be able to relax just by saying the word. My thoughts during this time are building a new memory for my cells.

How I see myself differently today is a much calmer self. Instead of giving off exuberant energy, I've learned to be quieter and conserve my internal energy for me. I'm learning daily to ask for help and express my needs. This has been the most challenging of my changes.

It's been three months and I feel I'm re-entering my world. It seems changes are ongoing, readjustments are facing me, and my body is still recovering.

Nada Deutsch

Specialization

Let me introduce myself to you. I was born and bred in India. From my childhood as far as I can recollect, the only serious diseases I ever heard of were that of typhoid and tuberculosis. Mostly these were fatal. Medicine had not advanced that much at that time. Regarding the word cancer, leave alone breast cancer, I had never heard of it. Usually this was kept a secret among close relations and friends. It was especially kept out of hearing of children.

There may be some reasons why at that time women rarely got breast cancer. Of course, I am referring to India from where I have come. Foremost what comes to my mind is that girls at that time were married at a very young age before they attained puberty. My own mother was married at the age of nine. By thirteen she gave birth to her first child. Secondly, there was breast feeding from the very next day the child was born. In view of this, mothers were given all good food and complete rest to keep mother and child healthy. Even poor families tried their best to follow the same system. Lastly, mothers were mostly given all herbal medicines after the delivery. This system still continues among those who want to stick to old customs. Later on as I grew up, reports started coming in the newspapers saying some communities were getting breast cancer, yet they did not know the cause.

Now coming to my own case. I am a three year survivor from breast cancer of the right breast. I am giving my experience so that my other women sisters should not make the same mistakes that I made, in spite of my being a literate person (I am a retired lawyer).

About five years ago, while still living in India, I felt a lump in my right breast. My internist sent me to have a mammogram which led to a needle biopsy because it looked suspicious. Test results came back as benign and I was so relieved. Yet about a week later, a family friend and

I discussed my situation and he immediately told me not to neglect the situation and recommended that I have the lump taken out. In spite of this advice I completely closed my mind to it. I kept complete trust in the benign test.

Soon after, I came to the U.S. to visit my daughter, who took me to a very good internist. It was recommended that I have another mammogram to compare the size from the old report. To my dismay, the lump had grown, the radiologist was 99% certain that the growth was malignant, and surgery was performed. I was then placed on tamoxifen. This was about eleven months from the first report.

Here I am, still alive, and I owe my life to the internist in the U.S. I am giving these details so that no one will repeat the mistakes I made. Self-examination is best and seeing a doctor who specializes in breast cancer should also not be put off. The sooner one gets rid of the lump, the more chances of ones survival.

Parvathi M. Heble

Empowerment

The shock of being diagnosed with cancer left me weak-kneed, feeling so vulnerable to a hostile invasion. This was NOT in my life-plan! One year a mammogram was clear. The next year I had a tumor three centimeters in size. It felt like a pink, pearl eraser lodged in my breast.

I had a wonderful team of doctors and, after much consultation, it was determined I needed a mastectomy followed by six months of chemotherapy. On the eve of the surgery, a friend called and told me the story of the Amazons from Greek Mythology. The strong and powerful Amazon women were known for their great feats of archery, and it is said they removed a breast in order to draw the bow more easily. Well, hearing this story suddenly straightened my weak knees and gave me a vision to latch onto. I was turned into a warrior woman, determined to win this battle! My surgery was done and I have been free of cancer for four years.

Feeling other women could be empowered by this myth, I designed a lapel pin and keychain which I distribute enclosed with the Amazon story. The design is a combination of a breast and the archer's bow. Some women have told me that to them it is as though the arrow is gliding through the breast killing off all disease. The connections I have made with women across the United States through this design have been truly rewarding. There is a vast network of support out there, growing day by day.

Jo Raksin

My Metamorphosis

From fog and shadow
and dimly lit awareness,
into black corners and hidden crannies,
I stumbled unknowingly along my darkened path
of indecision, fear, and doubt.

Abruptly, I *turned*
into my sun flooded field of open paths,
dancing with laughing buttercups,
ribbons of rainbows and angels afloat
streaming through my being.
Awake to life!

Anne DeWitt

And Share the Joy

How beautiful... the leaf!
I ask, "'Why can I enjoy its very existence
And know that others do not see and feel its presence?"
Because.

Because perhaps people have not learned to see.
They look but without comprehension.
Because perhaps man is caught up in this complex world and does not
take time to see how beautiful nature is.

To all. . .

Grasp! Grasp this precious opportunity.
Let yourself realize the beauty which abounds.
And as you look, see.
See each leaf as a unique entity as man is himself.

Become aware... aware of lines, shapes, designs and repetition in nature.
Be alone in nature for...just a brief moment.
Experience... and *share the joy!*

Jeannette K. Gardner

Ego

I am not a breast. My ego is not in my breast. My ego is in my whole person, in my soul. You might have to separate my body parts, but you can never hurt my soul. I am a woman and will always be one. Femininity is not measured by how many body parts you may or may not have, but rather by the person inside you. This can never be dissected out of your body. Breasts do not determine your femininity. Being female depends on how you think, act, and use your body to express your feelings. The "packaging" doesn't matter; it is what is inside that "mental box" and how it is used that makes you a totally sensual, alluring lady.

Miriam Handel

Contributions

by the
Loving Support Group

Love to ALL

It is hard to know sometimes why things happen to us the way they do. I have asked this question so many times throughout the last ten years. I am a person who has had many dear friends and family leave me due to cancer. Although I have never had to go through the shock and the pain of what my mom and my friends have had to deal with, a part of me has felt the anguish and the grief of what they have felt. So often I was either present when the news was given, assisting them with chemo treatments, or lending support to help them get back on their feet again. Thus the fear, the hurt, and even sometimes the anger is not foreign from my understanding.

Through these experiences I felt myself growing and learning that the most important and precious things in life **AREN'T THINGS!!!** Family, relationships with friends and God were the only real values, the ones you can only find through life's ups and downs.

I have had many say to me, "How could you stand to be there?" or "Isn't it depressing to go to the doctors and chemo treatments?" Sometimes it was! But I always felt that if I had those feelings, imagine how awful it was for them.

I remember someone telling me years ago that God will never give us more than we can bear. So I, too, try and pass those words along to the many wonderful friends who have had to deal with the awful disease. But know dear friends, that even though we do not walk in your shoes, we are hurting inside for you, too, and pray that only positive things will come and touch your heart and soul as so many of you have touched mine.

Cathy Thomas (Friend)

Hippity Hop

Hippity Hop through life.
Smile when the future looks blue.
Hold up your chin through thick and thin
And happiness will come to you.

John Keltus (Father)

Written in his daughter Mary Eileen Kennedy's autograph book when she was 12 years old

Beautiful Smile

Jeanette's good friend had been through breast cancer about five years before she started her treatments. This friend was an excellent source for strength, knowledge, and reassurance.

As for me, every time I looked at her I cried a little bit inside but I tried not to show it to her. After all, I had to be the macho man of the house, so I had to play the part.

Incredible how well she looked and how often she got compliments by total strangers when she wore her lady baseball caps that were studded with glass jewels. "You look so chic! Where did you get that hat?" they questioned. We would glance at one another and give each other the knowing look that people in harmony can give and receive. We would start laughing and that beautiful smile would return for those brief moments. She thought about how well she looked.

Alan Sherman (Husband)

Survivors' Tea

They chat in the lobby.
    At the Registration table.
Hug in front of the dessert cart
    Near the speakers podium.

Dainty hats bob across a sea of
    flowers, ribbons, china cups.
Those who wear them discuss
    recurrence, hair loss, lymph nodes.

The debate between saline and silicon rages
    over finger sandwiches.
Dark conversations thrash above our heads.
    They are like sharks with
    razor teeth ripping through a tranquil ocean
    surface,

But no one here is drowning.

Warriors in pink hats and patent leather shoes
    have jumped into the deep water.
They have emerged victorious
    from their battle with the churning surf.

I am not a member of this club.
        Do not wish to be.
Yet their spirit draws me in.
        Their strength inspires me.

I yearn to swim in their peaceful waters,
        To drift in the current of their wisdom.

To sail with the Survivors!

Lisa-Marie Pellegrino

Timing Is Everything

There was a moment when I was feeling about as low as I can remember. Awaiting my wife's surgery and while she was sedated, we were alone. Jeannette was sleeping. I was close to tears. My thoughts were that we didn't deserve this. Jeannette was too loving, too beautiful. Why?

Then, it happened. A gray haired lady approached me and extended her hand. She told me that she was a volunteer and that she would pray for us right then. The support that she gave, just at this time, was magical. How could it have come just at the time that we desperately needed it? We did deserve this love and this loving lady who volunteers. I was moved and will always be grateful. *Timing is everything.*

Jerry R. Gardner (Husband)

A Wonder to Realize

"Now, are you sure you want me to do this?"

"Yeah. It's falling out in clumps anyway," she said, wrinkling her nose. "It's too thin to style either."

Her thin, patched hair lay at my reluctant disposal. All those years of her bitching at me for cutting my own hair. . . It should've been a privilege, but I wanted to cry. All the universal signs of femininity, breasts and hair, were leaving her. She was mother to me, but suddenly older, grayer. Her body thinned before my eyes and frailty struck me. My rough hands through her scalp began to caress. Affection was showing in her son who loved to call her nicknames like "Big Brain" or "Beanpole" or "Retard." "Why now?"

Was she actually an object of respect and love in my life? Until then, my ridiculous panacea for mixed feelings was the emphasis for affection; hugs 'n kisses 'n hugs 'n kisses.

What a wonderful thing to realize that affection shows in very strange ways.

Her hair lay in a pile in the sink, and her head was a mess of shaved, uneven hairs.

"There. All done."

"I look like I'm a G.I.," she groaned.

I looked in the mirror. She was mother, but much older. A new kind of mother. Beautiful, too. I looked at myself. I was older. No longer a child. All these years of feeling perpetually fifteen years old must've fallen in the sink as well. Not a child but a young man.

And I was getting older by the second.

Christopher Allen (Son)

In Her Honor

It was April 12, Palm Sunday, the last day of my sister, Pene's 54th year on this earth. It was what she had prayed for near the end and what we, her family, feared, yet rejoiced in. "This day is sacred to the Lord. Do not fear, for the joy of the Lord is your strength" were verses from Nehemiah 8:10 that were given to me. We were there to the end. We bathed her, prepared her body for what was ahead of her. She opened her eyes to her twin Pam those last moments and then passed on to be met, as Max Lucado wrote, with the "applause of Heaven." Because of the constant presence throughout her illness of her family and friends, especially our mother, Audrey Jensen, and my sister, her identical twin, Pam Jensen Smith, we all realize that the strength and peace surrounding us came from the victory of God's promises and the victory of love. To honor my sister, Pene, I share my original poem, **The Lord is Your Shepard.**

The Lord is Your Shepherd

The Lord is your Shepherd. He takes care of His sheep;
Now gently He'll hold you, as you start your sleep.
He'll walk right beside you. He'll go all the way,
He'll fill you with His love and His peace today.

His arms will enfold you ... He holds close His own;
His focus is on you. you'll go to His throne.
He'll tell you of wonders you've questioned before...
He'll show you His glories, His secrets—and more.

He'll talk to you softly with praise for your life;
He knows all about you. He knows of your strife.
And He will reward you ... your job was well done;
You gave Him your life ... He gave you His Son.

You'll feel His strong presence. He'll take away fear...
O're death He's claimed victory, your Savior is here.
The Lord is your Shepherd... that's all that you need;
The Bread of Life, He is ... Today, you He'll feed.

His love's everlasting—His peace, always there;
For you are His treasure in Heaven so fair;
Know God's perfect timing will be His this day
When He takes your hand ... guides you ... the rest of the way.

Wendy Jensen Thomas
(Sister of Pene Jensen Church)

Together We Will Win

As the husband of a breast cancer patient, I have lived through the many highs and lows that my wife has faced since first being diagnosed with breast cancer. At first I was in denial. That kind of a thing could not happen to my wife. She had always kept herself healthy. There was no history of breast cancer in her family. Maybe the lump they found through mammography was not really cancer. She had a history of cysts which we had aspirated each time, but cancer, no, not her. She was too fragile. How would she be able to cope with the **"BIG C"**? But, it was not Janet who was in denial. It was me.

My wife made it through all of the surgeries, through all of the decisions, through all of the pain, through all of the uncertainties of a diagnosis of cancer. I was there in the beginning. I will remain there with her for as long as it takes to win the battle.

It is now nearly four years past the initial diagnosis. *Our lives have changed, but for the better. Each day is more precious. Each hour more important to us.* We have begun our journey through cancer and are now working with others to help them through their trials and tribulations with cancer. We are hoping to see the eradication of breast cancer as a threat to humanity in our lifetime. *Together we will win.*

Robert L. Butcher (Husband)

Bright Side

No one said life would be free of problems or pain.
No one said there would never be dark days or rain.
But just as the sun breaks through the clouds
And the flower sleeps beneath the frost,
Look at what you have left and not what you have
lost.

Carolyn Breen (Friend)

Dear Friends,

Don't grieve for me, for now I'm free;
I'm following the path God laid for me.
I took his hand when I heard him call;
I turned my back and left it all.

I could not stay another day,
To laugh, to love, to work, to play.
Tasks left undone must stay that way;
I found that place at the close of day.

If my parting has left a void,
Then fill it with remembered joy.
A friendship shared, a laugh, a kiss;
Ah, yes, these things, I too will miss.

Be not burdened with times of sorrow;
I wish you the sunshine of tomorrow.
My life's been full; I savored much;
Good friends, good times, a loved one's touch.

Perhaps my time seemed too brief;
Don't lengthen it now with undue grief.
Lift up your heart and share with me;
God wanted me now; He has set me free.

Author Unknown

Memorial Tribute to
Jana Kelly and Brenda Sach

Personal
Thoughts

www.ingramcontent.com/pod-product-compliance
Lightning Source LLC
Chambersburg PA
CBHW030759150426
42813CB00068B/3261/J